414

# Huckn...

*on old picture po...*

OTTEWELL, DAVID
HUCKNALL ON OLD PICTURE POSTCARDS

**1.** A love... ...vered
cart trun... ...posite
*way som...*

CENTRAL GROUP

Notti...

£5.50

## Designed and Published by
## Reflections of a Bygone Age,
## Keyworth, Nottingham

### ISBN 0 946245 87 8

*First published November 1994*
*Revised and reprinted 1995, 1996, 1998,*
*2000 and March 2003*

## Printed by
## Adlard Print and Typesetting Services,
## Ruddington, Notts.

**1a.** A flooded Portland Road on 1st June 1908, featured on a postcard by an anonymous publisher. A horse and rider, along with a delivery cart, can be seen in the distance, but the chances of the watching crowd going anywhere look remote! The postcard was obviously bought by a visitor at the time, as it was eventually posted at Horwich, Lancashire - but not until September 1911!

ST. JOHN'S CHURCH. HUCKNALL TORKARD.

**2.** Standing at the Bulwell end of the town, St. John's Church was opened in 1877 at a cost of over £1,000. This postcard was no. 637 in the 'Clumber' series, published by Albert Hindley.

BUTLERS HILL HUCKNALL

**3.** This anonymously-published card, sent from Hucknall in June 1905, shows the Hicks Memorial School on Butler's Hill, built just beyond St. John's Church in 1878. Note the horse-droppings indicating the type of traffic dominating the road!

# INTRODUCTION

1994 sees the centenary of picture postcards in Britain although their popularity did not really take off until 1902 when the message was allowed to be written on the reverse with the address. The hundred years of picture postcards have provided us with a wealth of views from which to choose a selection for this book.

Local publishers like W. North and P.A. Bullock of Hucknall, plus C. & A.G. Lewis and Alfred Hindley (Clumber series) from Nottingham are featured in these pages as well as firms from further afield like The Doncaster Rotophoto Co. and Valentine of Dundee. These publishers have provided an extensive and varied coverage of subjects in Hucknall.

Although Hucknall has only played a minor part on the national stage (the birthplace of the composer Eric Coates and the last resting place of the poet Byron being examples) it has nevertheless its own distinctive history which has touched the lives of many.

I hope that the illustrations in the book will help to take you on a trip down memory lane.

**David Ottewell**
**November 1994**

*Acknowledgements:* I should like to thank Eric Horriben and Maureen Newton for advice and information.

*Front cover:* High Street from Market Place, with Green's monument on the left. 'Peveril' series card, posted to Shirebrook in July 1919.

**4.** Portland Road, Hucknall, on a 'Rex' series postcard sent to Halifax in November 1928. The "Yew Tree Hotel", featured on the left, was built in the early 19th century to replace a pub of the same name which was situated about 150 yards further up Beardall Street.

**5.** This card was sent from Hucknall in 1913, and shows an impressive gathering outside the "Yew Tree Hotel" on Portland Road. The placards being held are for the *Daily Citizen,* which advertises that it is *"the mouthpiece of labour"*, *"the champion of the railwaymen,"* and exhorts workers to *"wake up and buy the Daily Citizen"*.

**6.** Looking away from Hucknall towards Bulwell, the photographer on this 'Rex' series card has captured Portland Road on a quiet occasion with no pedestrians in sight. In the distance, the first shop is displaying a sign for Lifebuoy soap. The card was postally used in September 1935.

**7.** A view looking down Watnall Road towards the High Street. The buildings on the left, including beer retailer James Saxton at no.86, have now gone, but the row of cottages beyond them remains, as does the building containing Palmer's cash drapery stores (built in 1895), though the roof has been flattened, and a furniture shop now operates from the premises. Postcard in the 'Peveril' series.

**8.** An early postcard of a similar view a little further down Watnall Road. It was posted from Hucknall in October 1904.

**9.** Zachariah Green was born on 5th May 1817, the son of a Napoleonic war medical orderly. He learned his medical skills from his father, and healed many in the town, gaining widespread respect. This 'Clumber' series card shows his cottage on Beardall Street. The postcard was sent to Retford in December 1908.

**10.** A postcard published by Valentine of Dundee in the 1950s shows the "Byron" picture house on the left. Posters on the wall advertise forthcoming films including *Gunsmoke, King Creole* (with Elvis Presley) and *Mardi Gras* (starring Pat Boone). A branch of the Hucknall Co-op is on the right.

**11.** Standing at the junction with Watnall Road, the photographer for the Doncaster Rotophoto Co. has taken a photo of High Street looking towards the Byron cinema. To the right we see the shops of W.R. Alcock, confectioner, at no. 31a, followed by Woods (drapers), Barkers (selling Cadbury's chocolate) and John Henry Vann, butchers, at no.25. A signpost on the lamp standard points the way to the Great Central Railway Station, placing the card around 1920-22. *(see illus.1 for a view looking the opposite way some 15 years earlier).*

High Street, Hucknall. No. 996.

**12.** Looking the opposite way to the previous card, this 1924-used postcard – sent to Southend – shows George J. Mason Ltd., provisions dealer, at no.31 advertising Hovis bread. As can be seen, there were few motor vehicles in the town in this era. Just beyond the cyclists is the start of Watnall Road. The postcard was published by C. & A.G. Lewis, Nottingham's best-known card producers, who were responsible for thousands of photographic cards locally and regionally.

HIGH STREET HUCKNALL TORKARD

**13.** A 'Peveril' series card, sent from Hucknall to Cheetham (Manchester) in July 1907, showing the Young Mens Christian Association building in the centre with striped blinds above the pavement. The boy in the foreground appears to be collecting recent horse droppings.

**14.** A view taken about 25 years after the previous illustration shows Walter Pepper's newsagent shop at 50 High Street, with a wide range of advertisement boards. Horse and cart has given way to the motor vehicle. The buildings on the immediate left, including the YMCA, have now, sadly, all been demolished.

**15.** A superb view on a postcard by C. & A.G. Lewis in their 'Robin Hood' series, showing the Coffee Tavern centre left. This was built by public subscription in 1884, designed by eminent local architect Watson Fothergill. The Tavern was flanked by Boots cash chemists (no.54) and Mary J. Anderson (milliner) at no. 56.

**16.** 'Clumber' series card sent from Hucknall to Bulwell in November 1905. The Coffee Tavern is again featured, but in this much earlier view, its neighbours were differently occupied. Nearest the camera was W. Burton, printer. The Tavern was a strictly temperance meeting place, used by many including miners' officials. The photographer has captured a selection of locals including a postman (2nd right).

**17.** A much later (1960s) postcard of this part of High Street showing a more garish Boots frontage. The bottom on the Coffee Tavern was converted into shops in the 1930s and is seen here occupied by Frank Sissons (electricals) and Wakefields. The "Red Lion" can be seen in the distance.

**18.** A superb photographic card of about 1908 showing horse-drawn transport, and looking towards the Parish Church. Titchfield Street runs off to the right beyond the shop blind.

**19.** Another view of the corner of High Street and Titchfield Street, this time on a Doncaster Rotophoto Co. card of about 1921. George Orme and sons' clothiers shop is on the left. Plenty of cyclists in evidence, but no motor vehicles!

High Street, Hucknall Notts

**20.** This postcard was sent by a Mrs. Noble to a friend in Wellingborough in December 1906. On it she notes *"I have got my number back at the Co-op"*. Other shops on this card are Prosser's, a Dining and Tea Rooms, Herbert Motors, F.E. Teed, and Herbert Walker newsagents.

HIGH ST & CHURCH. HUCKNALL TORKARD.

**21.** Looking towards the church and Market Place in 1907 on a 'Clumber' series postcard showing the "Mason's Arms" on the right. This building – and the ones beyond and opposite – have been converted or rebuilt as shop premises.

MARKET PLACE HUCKNALL TORKARD

**22.** This 'Clumber' series card was sent from Hucknall in October 1906 by Clara, who was staying in the nurses' home, Hucknall Torkard. The photograph was taken from the Market Place, and looking down High Street, we can see a crowd of children gathered in front of the Green Memorial. Turner & Son's horse-drawn bakery van has stopped to be part of the picture.

**23.** A much more recent (early 1960s) view of High Street, published by Valentine of Dundee. Redevelopment has taken place on the right, leaving it much as it is today. The left has also been drastically changed at the Market Place end in the name of progress.

**24.** An impressive gathering in Market Place about 1920, complete with brass band. The Free Library is decorated for the occasion and there is a significant military presence by the Green Monument.

**25.** A view taken from the "Half Moon Hotel" looking across the Market Place and Baker Street. Co-operative House (now vacant) can be seen in the distance on this 1960s card published by Valentine of Dundee. A parked van advertises 'Lyons Swiss Rolls'.

**26.** When Zachariah Green died on 22nd January 1897, £400 was raised by public subscription for a memorial. This took the form of a fountain in red and grey Scottish granite which was erected in the Market Place. C. & A.G. Lewis 'Robin Hood' series postcard of about 1920.

**27.** A marvellously-animated picture of Hucknall's H drawn transport. Red Lion Yard is through the curve street towards the Market Place. The photographer who he was.

bout 1910 showing a variety of horse-drawn and hand-
n the right, and "The Mason's Arms" is further down the
sponsible for this card (and no.18) gave no indication of


-19-

Hucknall Church

**28.** St. Mary Magdalene Church, Hucknall, is prominently situated overlooking the Market Place. The poet Byron, who died in April 1824, was buried here. Doubts about the authenticity of this claim led in June 1938 to the vicar, T.G. Barber, and others, opening the vault to examine Byron's body which was found to be perfectly preserved.

**29.** Stone-laying at the Godber Memorial Church Hall in October 1906.

Memorial Pulpit at Hucknall Church.

**30.** Hucknall Church's memorial pulpit seen on a postcard sent to London in December 1905.

**31.** The statue of the poet Lord Byron in the central niche of what was Co-operative House *(see illus. 25)*. The poet, whose family home was at nearby Newstead Abbey, died in Greece in 1824. The statue was erected by Elias Lacey.

**32.** A postcard view of Baker Street *(see illus. 25)* published by the Doncaster Rotophoto Co. with Mrs. Ellen Taylor's fishmongers shop prominent. Further along can be seen signs for E. Morley Robinson (boot factor) and William Taylder and Sons (clothiers).

**33.** The Free Library was designed by A.N. Bromley in the Queen Anne style, and opened in 1887. It cost £2,000, which was donated by J.E. Ellis and H.B.Paget. This postcard, by an anonymous publisher, was sent to an address in Co-operative Avenue, Hucknall, from Derby in August 1904.

**34.** Coronation celebrations on Watnall Road, Hucknall, on a postcard published by Walter North of Portland Road. The view is looking down towards High Street.

Baker Street, Hucknall

**35.** A 1950s period card published by A.W. Bourne of Leicester. The photo was taken from the Market Place, showing the United Methodist (Trinity) church, with W. Taylder and Co.'s clothes shop next to it (now 'Motor World'). From 1963 this has been the Central Methodist Church, and has had the facade rebuilt.

**36.** A group of local children pose for an anonymous photographer in the middle of Carlingford Road about 1910. Beyond them can be seen Holy Cross Catholic Church and the School, which were built in 1886.

**37.** This postcard in the 'Peveril Real Photo' series shows the "Pilot Palace" cinema, facing what was in 1920 a Methodist New Connection Chapel but which is now, incongruously, the "Lord Byron" pub. The roof of the Wesleyan Reform Church, built in 1906, can just be seen beyond the "Palace".

**38.** The Duke of Portland, the principal landowner in the area, gave his name to the "Portland Arms" on Annesley Road as well as to a major thoroughfare on the other side of the town. 'Peveril' series card, published about 1905.

ANNESLEY RD HUCKNALL

**39.** A photographic card of similar vintage to the previous illustration, but looking the opposite way down Annesley Road. The "Portland Arms" is now on the left, advertising Shipstone's Ales and Stout in the windows. Nearer to the camera on the

same side is William Hanford's drapers shop at no.38. The cart on the right belongs to William Wyld of Eastwood. Note the three balls sign for the pawnbroker's.

CLUB MILL, HUCKNALL TORKARD.

**40.** The Hucknall Sick Club erected the Club Mill on Bulwell Lane in 1791. It was, however, a poor site for catching the wind, and in 1826 the mill was dismantled and moved to Sandy Lane, as seen here on this 'Clumber' series postcard, sent from Hucknall to Aslockton in March 1910.

THE OLD MILL, HUCKNALL 568-5

**41.** The Club Mill prospered on its new site on Sandy Lane, though when the Great Central Railway reached the town, it was proposed to demolish it. However, a compromise was reached, and the new railway by-passed the mill. This postcard view was published in 1920 by the Doncaster Rotophoto Co.

**42.** A branch line of the Midland Counties Railway linking Mansfield with London came through Hucknall. It was opened in 1848. Postcard in the 'Peveril' series, published about 1910. The station, later re-named Hucknall Byron, accommodated some seventeen passenger trains in each direction (three extra on Saturdays) at the time the card was published. It was closed to passenger traffic in October 1964 and the station buildings subsequently demolished. A new, more functional, building was erected for the re-opening of the station in 1993 as part of the new Robin Hood Line development.

**43.** Hucknall Town Station in the late 1920s. On the Great Northern line between Nottingham and Shirebrook, it had at least ten trains in each direction calling daily in 1910, but passenger traffic declined dramatically, and services ended in September 1931. Goods trains used it until 1965. Card by Douglas Thompson.

**44.** Hucknall Central on a photographic card published by Douglas Thompson in 1951. This was the town's main line station, on the London (Marylebone) – Sheffield Great Central. It remained open for both passengers and freight until October 1963.

**45.** Hucknall aerodrome was opened in July 1916. It served in both world wars, but its claim to aeronautical history lies in its association with Rolls Royce, who moved into hangers here in 1934. They developed prototype engines like the Merlin and prototype aeroplanes such as the vertical take-off jet which started life as 'the flying bedstead'. 'Rex' series card from the mid-1920s.

**46.** Walter Syson of Hucknall was a very adventurous person, travelling the world trying to make his fortune. Closer to home about 1935, he is seen here leading his local scout troop on Bottom Common off Nabbs Lane. An Imperial Airways bi-plane is the source of interest here.

**47.** The Duke of Portland gave 11 acres of land to set up this park, named after his son, the Marquis of Titchfield, who performed the opening ceremony in July 1922. The lake was added in 1925, but was filled in after subsidence damage in 1946. Postcard by J.T. Davenport, posted from Hucknall in December 1927.

**48.** Zachariah Green's monument was eventually moved from the Market Place to the more spacious Titchfield Park. Part of the inscription reads *"he spent his life in alleviating the suffering of his fellow men."*

**49.** One of the members of Hucknall's Excelsior Brass Band *(see illus. 55)* was Jimmy Salt, seen here in the late 1920s. He was an all-England trombone champion. Card published by P.A. Bullock of Hucknall and Kirkby.

**50.** A 1960s view of the bowling green in Titchfield Park.

**51.** W. North of Hucknall published this card showing the unveiling of the town's war memorial in Titchfield Park on 3rd September 1922. Brigadier-general Sir J.F. Laycock K.C.M.G., D.S.O performed the ceremony, while the dedication service was conducted by Rev. Canon Barber.

**52.** Hucknall's two collieries were first sunk in 1861 and 1865 respectively. No.2, featured here, was closed in 1986 as part of a widespread shutdown of Nottinghamshire pits in the middle of that decade.

UCKNALL N?2 COLLIERY

**53.** Another W. North postcard, this time featuring Butlers Hill Primitive Methodist F.C. in the 1921-2 season. According to the reverse of the card, the team were *"runners-up, same points as Daybrook."*

**54.** Butlers Hill infant school *(see illus.3)* was opened in February 1877 when 100 children were admitted. A new block was built on Bestwood Road to accommodate a much larger number of pupils in 1893. Here is Group 4 in 1915 – a very mixed bunch!